D1346432

The Little Book of Rebels

The Little Book of Rebels

First published in the UK by
New Internationalist Publications Ltd., Oxford, England.

Printed on recycled paper by C&C Offset Printing Co. Ltd., Hong Kong.
Designed by Ian Nixon

British Library Cataloguing-in-Publication Data.
A catalogue record for this book is available from the British Library.

ISBN 1 869847 98 9

New Internationalist Publications Ltd.
Registered Office: 55 Rectory Road, Oxford OX4 1BW

www.newint.org

HE LITTLE BOOK OF

REBELS

Compiled by Vanessa Baird

For all rebels at heart

Foreword

Don't whatever you do read this book. In fact, it should probably go out with a 'government health warning'.

Contained herein are the subversive, wilful, frivolous, provocative words of rebels from all over the world.

There's Subcomandante Marcos who's condemning globalization from the Mexican jungles of Chiapas; Indian activist Medha Paktar defying, to death if need be, the Narmada Dam project; and French anti-corporate farmer José Bové realizing the dreams of many as he dumps manure on McDonald's.

Not to mention old troublemakers from the past, like Jesus, Che, Gandhi and Pankhurst.

How do you identify a rebel? Well, they tend to have a view of the world that departs from the accepted norm. Furthermore, they are not happy with things as they are. They want to change them. Not only that, they think they *can* change them. They are often courageous to an unreasonable degree. And very often they just don't seem able to take authority seriously.

Really, you must not read this book! It might give you ideas.

Vanessa Baird

Feet and knees

Better to die on your feet than live on your knees.

Emiliano Zapata (1879-1919), Mexican revolutionary.

Hope

To be truly radical is to make hope possible rather than despair convincing.

Raymond Williams (1921-1989), Welsh novelist, critic and founder of the 'cultural materialism' approach to literature.

Bombs and brains

If protesting against having a nuclear bomb implanted in my brain is anti-Hindu and anti-national, then I secede. I hereby declare myself an independent, mobile republic. I am a citizen of the earth. I own no territory. I have no flag. I'm female, but I have nothing against eunuchs. My policies are simple. I'm willing to sign any nuclear nonproliferation treaty or nuclear test ban treaty that's going. Immigrants are welcome. You can help me design our flag.

Arundhati Roy (b. 1961), Indian novelist and essayist, author of *The God of Small Things* and *The End of Imagination*.

Size

If you think you are too small to make a difference try sleeping with a mosquito.

Dalai Lama (b 1935), Tenzin Gyatso, temporal and
spiritual leader of Tibet.

Never doubt that a small group of thoughtful committed citizens can change the world. Indeed it's the only thing that ever has.

Margaret Mead (1901-1978), US anthropologist,
outspoken on issues of women's rights, birth control
and the environment.

GM Food

Yes... I participated in the destruction of genetically modified maize, which was stored in Novartis' grain silos in Nerac. And the only regret I have now is that I wasn't able to destroy more of it.

José Bové, contemporary, French farmer, trade unionist and direct-action campaigner against GM and 'McDonaldization', speaking during his trial.

Appearances

Nail polish or false eyelashes isn't politics. If you have good politics, what you wear is irrelevant. I don't take dictation from the pig-o-cratic style-setters who say I should dress like a middle-aged colored lady. My politics don't depend on whether my tits are in or out of a bra.

Florynce R Kennedy (1916-2001), US Lawyer and civil-rights activist. Outspoken champion of African Americans, women, the poor, homosexuals and prostitutes.

If you want to say something radical, you should dress conservative.

Steve Biko (1946-77), South African anti-apartheid activist, murdered in police custody.

We are indigenous

Today we say we are indigenous, and we
say it like giants.
Today, 503 years after death from a
foreign land arrived to bring us silence,
we resist and we speak.
Today, 503 years later, we live…
Long live the indigenous Mexicans!
Democracy!
Liberty!
Justice!

Subcomandante Marcos, contemporary, rebel leader
of Zapatista National Liberation Army.

Media

No self-respecting fish would be wrapped in a Murdoch newspaper.

Mike Royko (1932-97), US journalist who resigned from the Chicago *Sun-Times* in 1984 when the paper was sold to Australian media mogul Rupert Murdoch.

Dam-busters

It is our pledge to face the water if it rises in the fields and houses... this is a very critical fight. A fight to the finish. Not because we want to commit suicide, but to save life.

Medha Paktar (b. 1955), Indian activist and environmentalist spearheading the campaign of Indian villagers against the Narmada Dam project.

Free speech

What is freedom of expression? Without freedom to offend it does not exist.

Salman Rushdie (b. 1947), Indian-born novelist, subjected to a fatwa or death sentence issued by Iran's Ayatollah Khomeini for the book *Satanic Verses*.

DIY

I tell women: 'Go and masturbate! Get loads of kinky books and masturbate every day!' They [men] do it from the age of nine!

Björk (b. 1965), Icelandic singer.

Rules

Britain does not rule the waves
She simply waives the bloody rules!

Steven Berkoff (b. 1937), British playwright,
actor and director, in his satire of the
Falklands War, *Sink the Belgrano!*

Perspectives

From the point of view of the Indians of the Caribbean islands, Christopher Columbus, with his plumed cap and red velvet cape, was the biggest parrot they had ever seen… From the point of view of the natives, it's the tourists who are picturesque.

Eduardo Galeano (b. 1940), Uruguayan historian, essayist and author of _Upside Down_.

AIDS

Societies need to have one illness which becomes identified with evil, and attaches blame to its 'victims'.

Susan Sontag (b. 1933), US critic and author.
Her books include *AIDS and Its Metaphors*.

Lies

In our country the lie has become not just a moral category but a pillar of the State.

Alexander Solzhenitsyn (b. 1918), Russian dissident who spent eight years in prison for criticizing Stalin. Finally exiled after publication of his book *The Gulag Archipelago*.

Sex

The only unnatural sex act is that which you cannot perform.

Alfred Kinsey (1894-1956), US zoologist
and sex researcher.

Greed

Beware, and be on your guard against every form of greed; for not even when one has an abundance does his life consist of his possessions.

Jesus of Nazareth (00-33 AD), rebellious Jewish prophet, champion of the oppressed, scourge of the rich, founder of Christianity.

The impossible

If we don't do the impossible, we shall be faced with the unthinkable.

Petra Kelly (1947-92), German politician, anti-nuclear activist and co-founder of the Green Party.

God

I cannot believe in a God who wants to be praised all the time.

Friedrich Nietzsche (1844-1900), German philosopher, author of *Beyond Good and Evil*.

Hey, let's get serious... God knows what he's doin'. He wrote this book here. An' the book says: 'He made us all to be just like Him.' So... If we're dumb... Then God is dumb... (An' maybe even a little ugly on the side).

Frank Zappa (1940-93), US alternative rock musician and satirist.

God is voluptuous and delicious.

Meister Eckhart (1260-1327), German theologian, writer and mystic.

Insurance

For almost seventy years now the life insurance industry has been a smug sacred cow feeding the public a steady line of sacred bull.

Ralph Nader (b. 1934), US consumer-rights activist and Green Party presidential candidate.

Marijuana

Is marijuana addictive? Yes, in the sense that most of the really pleasant things in life are worth endlessly repeating.

Richard Neville (b. 1941), Australian journalist, charged and imprisoned in the UK for publishing a magazine (*Oz*) likely to corrupt public morals.

People and animals

The animals of the world exist for their own reasons. They were not made for humans any more than black people were made for white, or women created for men.

Alice Walker (b. 1944), US novelist, activist and critic.
Author of *The Color Purple*.

Vegetarianism brings with it a new relationship to food, plants and nature. Flesh taints our meals. Disguise it as we may, the fact remains that the centerpiece of our dinner has come to us from the slaughterhouse, dripping blood.

Peter Singer (b. 1946) Australian philosopher and
author of the groundbreaking *Animal Liberation*.

Genitals

You don't need genitals for politics. You need brains.

Shabnam Nehru, contemporary, Indian politician, municipal councilor for Hisar and first member of the outcaste *hijra* (eunuch) community to run for Parliament.

A great poem

Love the earth and sun and animals, despise riches, give alms to every one that asks, stand up for the stupid and crazy, devote your income and labour to others, hate tyrants, argue not concerning God, have patience and indulgence toward the people, take off your hat to nothing known or unknown… re-examine all you have been told at school or church or in any book, dismiss whatever insults your own soul, and your very flesh shall be a great poem and have the richest fluency.

Walt Whitman (1819-92), US poet,
author of *Leaves of Grass*.

Rewards

The salary of the chief executive of the large corporations is not a market reward for achievement. It is frequently in the nature of a warm personal gesture by the individual to himself.

JK Galbraith (b. 1908), Canadian-born economist, author of *The Affluent Society*.

When a man tells you that he got rich through hard work, ask him whose.

Don Marquis (1878-1937), US humourist and journalist.

Refugees

You can judge politicians by how they treat refugees; they do to them what they would like to do to everyone else if they could get away with it.

Ken Livingstone (b. 1945), maverick left-wing British MP, expelled from the Labour party in 2000 when he ran for Mayor of London as an independent – and won.

Male divinity

If God is male, the male is God. The divine patriarch castrates women as long as he is allowed to live on in the human imagination.

Mary Daly (b. 1928), US writer, theologian and radical feminist, author of many books including *Pure Lust: Elemental Feminist Philosophy*.

Nationalism

Patriotism is the virtue of the vicious.

Oscar Wilde (1854-1900), Irish-born wit, playwright,
imprisoned for his homosexuality.

Nationalism is an infantile sickness. It is
the measles of the human race.

Albert Einstein (1879-1955) Austrian-born physicist and
pacifist, developer of the *Theory of Relativity*.

Shell on trial

I and my colleagues here are not the only ones on trial. Shell is here on trial... the company has indeed ducked this particular trial, but its day will surely come.

Ken Saro Wiwa (1941-95), Nigerian writer and activist leader of the Ogoni people who were protesting against Shell's oil exploration on their land, environmental destruction and human-rights abuses. Saro Wiwa was executed with eight others by the Nigerian Government.

Reasonableness

We are the wrong people of
the wrong skin in the wrong
continent and what in hell is everyone
being reasonable about.

June Jordan (b. 1936), US poet writing in
Poem About My Rights.

Economics

 What is economics? A science invented by the upper class in order to acquire the fruits of the labour of the underclass.

August Strindberg (1849-1912), Swedish dramatist.

 Call a thing immoral or ugly, soul-destroying or a degradation of man, a peril to the peace of the world or to the well-being of future generations; as long as you have not shown it to be 'uneconomic' you have not really questioned its right to exist, grow, and prosper.

E F Schumacher (1911-77), German-born economist and author of *Small is Beautiful: Economics as if People Mattered*.

The joy of rebellion

Revolution is the festival of the oppressed.

Germaine Greer (b. 1939), Australian-born feminist
writer and critic. Author of the groundbreaking
The Female Eunuch.

Parental guidance

I have told my sons that they are not under any circumstances to take part in massacres, and that the news of massacres of enemies is not to fill them with satisfaction and glee. I have also told them not to work for companies which make massacre machinery, and to express contempt for people who think we need machinery like that.

Kurt Vonnegut (b. 1922), US novelist writing in *Slaughterhouse-Five*.

Colonial counsel

It is easier for the proverbial camel to pass through the needle's eye, hump and all, than for an erstwhile colonial administration to give sound and honest counsel of a political nature to its liberated territory.

Kwame Nkrumah (1909-72), called the 'Gandhi of Africa', who led the Gold Coast's struggle for independence, becoming first Prime Minister of Ghana (1957-60).

Power and privilege

What power have you got? Where did you get it from? In whose interests do you exercise it? To whom are you accountable? How do we get rid of you?

Tony Benn (b. 1925), left-wing British Labour MP.
The above are questions he habitually asks
on meeting someone with power.

Labels

I came to live in a country I love; some people label me a defector. I have loved men and women in my life; I've been labelled a 'bisexual defector' in print. I don't like labels. Just call me Martina.

Martina Navratilova (b. 1956), Czech-born US tennis player, outspoken on a number of issues including gay and animal rights and the status of women in tennis.

Religion

Religion is the frozen thought of men out of which they build temples.

> **Jiddu Krishnamurti** (1895-1986), Indian spiritual philosopher.

Any God I ever felt in church, I brought in with me.

> **Alice Walker** (b. 1944), US novelist and activist.

Revolt

A riot is at bottom the language of the unheard.

Martin Luther King (1929-68), US civil-rights leader.

A little rebellion now and then is a good thing.

Thomas Jefferson (1743-1826), American independence leader and President.

Culture

When we were at school we were taught to sing the songs of the Europeans. How many of us were taught the songs of the Wanyamwezi or of the Wahehe? Many of us have learnt to dance the *rumba*, or the *cha-cha-cha*, to rock and roll, and to twist and even to waltz and foxtrot. But how many of us can dance, or have even heard of the *gombe sugu*, the *mangala*, *nyang'umumi*, *kiduo*, or *lele mama*?

Julius Nyerere (1922-99), Tanzanian liberation leader who became the independent country's first president in 1964.

Corporatism

Our civilization is locked in the grip of an ideology – corporatism. An ideology that denies and undermines the legitimacy of individuals as the citizen in a democracy. The particular imbalance of this ideology leads to a worship of self-interest and a denial of the public good. The practical effects on the individual are passivity and conformism in the areas that matter, and non-conformism in the areas that don't.

John Ralson Saul (b. 1947), Canadian novelist, essayist and commentator.

Holy condoms

I hang on to my Catholicism by a tiny thread. I'm still looking for something in the sacred text that prohibits using condoms.

Paul Farmer, contemporary, radical US doctor, founder of Partners in Health in Haiti.

Race

*B*e nice to the whites, they need you to rediscover their humanity.

Desmond Tutu (b. 1931), South Africa's first black bishop, dedicated to the struggle for a democratic, just and non-racial South Africa. Chair of the Truth and Reconciliation Committee.

Laws

The more corrupt the state, the more numerous the laws.

Tacitus (56–115 AD), Roman senator and historian.

An individual who breaks a law that conscience tells him is unjust, and willingly accepts the penalty... to arouse the conscience of the community over its injustice, is... expressing the very highest respect for law.

Dr Martin Luther King (1929-68), US church minister and civil-rights leader.

Consuming passions

In a consumer society there are inevitably two kinds of slaves; the prisoners of addiction and the prisoners of envy.

Ivan Illich (b. 1926), Austrian-born philosopher, theologian and author of *Limits to Medicine*.

Disobedience

I am a disobedient person. I have never obeyed the customs of any society. I have never obeyed the laws of the state. Rejecting everything, unmanageable, untamable – I have always followed my own momentum. Why? The answer lies in my feeling that the discriminatory treatment of women in my society is inhuman...

Taslima Nasrin (b. 1962), Bangladeshi novelist and poet who has come under a fatwa for her book *Shame*. She lives in hiding in exile.

Disobedience is the true foundation of liberty. The obedient must be slaves.

Henry David Thoreau (1817-62), US essayist, poet and naturalist.

Change

You have to be the change you want to see in the world.

Mahatma Gandhi (1869-1948), Indian independence
leader, lawyer and pacifist.

Hitherto philosophers have only interpreted the world, the point however is to change it.

Karl Marx (1818-83), German political theorist and
co-author of the *Communist Manifesto*.

Superpower 1

Pillagers of the world, [the Romans] have exhausted the land by their indiscriminate plunder, and now they ransack the sea. A rich enemy excites their cupidity; a poor one, their lust for power... They are the only people on earth to whose covetousness both riches and poverty are equally tempting. To robbery, butchery, and rapine, they give the lying name of 'government'; they create a desolation and call it peace.

Tacitus (56-115 AD), Roman senator and historian.

Superpower 2

America is gangsterism for the private profit of the few.

Vanessa Redgrave, contemporary, British-born actor and political activist.

Aristocracy

Not a reluctant peer but a persistent commoner.

Tony Benn (b. 1925), British leftist MP who gave up his peerage to enter the House of Commons. He has repeatedly campaigned for the abolition of the House of Lords, the unelected second chamber of Parliament.

Incitement

There is something that governments care for far more than human life, and that is the security of property, and so it is through property that we shall strike the enemy... Be militant each in your own way. And my last word is to the Government: I incite this meeting to rebellion... Take me if you dare.

Emmeline Pankhurst (1858-1928), English suffragist and campaigner for women's votes and rights.

Schizophrenia

The experience and behaviour that gets labelled schizophrenic is a special strategy that person invents in order to live an unlivable situation.

RD Laing (1927-89), unorthodox Scottish psychiatrist and author of *The Politics of Experience*.

Faith

I began revolution with 82 men. If I had [to] do it again, I'd do it with 10 or 15 and absolute faith.

Fidel Castro (b. 1926), Cuban revolutionary who ousted President Batista in 1959.

Family life

However sugarcoated and ambiguous, every form of authoritarianism must start with a belief in some group's greater right to power, whether that right is justified by sex, race, class, religion, or all four. However far it may expand, the progression inevitably rests on unequal power and airtight roles within the family.

Gloria Steinem (b. 1934), US feminist writer, editor, and co-founder of *MS* magazine.

Providing for one's family is a watertight excuse for making money hand over fist. Greed may be a sin, exploitation of other people might look rather nasty, but who can blame a man 'doing the best' for his children.

Eva Figes (b. 1932), Anglo-German writer, translator and feminist critic.

Capitalism

Capitalism is the astounding belief that the wickedest of men will do the wickedest of things for the greatest good of everyone.

John Maynard Keynes (1883-1946), British economist, influential pioneer of macroeconomics. He favoured government spending as a cure for rising unemployment.

Women's liberation

I didn't fight to get women out from behind the vacuum cleaner to get them onto the board of Hoover.

Gemaine Greer (b. 1939), Australian-born feminist, academic and writer.

Right to choose

If I cannot give my consent to my own death, then whose body is this? Who owns my life?

Sue Rodriguez (1951-94), Canadian activist for the legalization of assisted suicide.

Action

Action! Action! not criticism, is the plain duty of this hour. The office of speech now is only to point out when, where, and how to strike to the best advantage.

> **Marcus Garvey** (1887-1940), Jamaican-born activist, Pan-Africanist and internationalist.

Don't agonize, organize.

> **Florynce Kennedy** (1916-2001), US lawyer, feminist, and civil-rights activist.

Inequality

I never could believe that Providence had sent a few men into the world, ready booted and spurred to ride, and millions ready saddled and bridled to be ridden.

Richard Rumbold (1622-1685), English republican who conspired to assassinate King Charles II. He spoke these words on the gallows.

Speaking out

We who have a Voice must be a Voice for the Voiceless!

Oscar Romero (1917-80), El Salvadorean Archbishop of San Salvador who was assassinated for speaking out against government-sanctioned death squad activities.

Fundamentalism

Truly this has been an age of
Ayatollahs, in which a phalanx of
guardians (Khomeini, the Pope, Margaret
Thatcher) simplify and protect one or
another creed, essence, primordial faith.
One fundamentalism invidiously attacks
the others in the name of sanity, freedom
and goodness.

Edward Said (b. 1935), Palestinian-born US social
and literary critic and commentator on
Middle Eastern issues.

Homosexuality

Y ou're neither unnatural, nor abominable, nor mad; you're as much a part of what people call nature as anyone else; only you're unexplained as yet – you've not got your niche in creation.

Radclyffe Hall (1883-1943), British author of the groundbreaking novel *The Well of Loneliness* which was banned for 'obscenity'.

M y lesbianism is an act of Christian charity. All those women out there are praying for a man, and I'm giving them my share.

Rita Mae Brown (b. 1944), US humourist and writer.

Property

The first man who, having fenced off a plot of land, thought of saying, 'This is mine' and found people simple enough to believe him was the real founder of civil society. How many crimes, wars, murders, how many miseries and horrors might the human race had been spared by the one who, upon pulling up the stakes or filling in the ditch, had shouted to his fellow men: 'Beware of listening to this impostor; you are lost if you forget the fruits of the earth belong to all and that the earth belongs to no one.'

Jean-Jacques Rousseau (1712-78), French philosopher and author of *Discourse on Inequality*.

Fear

Our deepest fear is not that we are inadequate. Our deepest fear is that we are powerful beyond measure. It is our light, not our darkness that most frightens us. We ask ourselves, who am I to be brilliant, gorgeous, talented and fabulous? Actually, who are you NOT to be?

Nelson Mandela (b. 1918), South African leader of the anti-apartheid movement. He spent 26 years in prison for his part in the banned African National Congress, then became South Africa's first black president in 1994.

Housework

There is no need to do any housework at all. After the first four years the dirt doesn't get any worse.

Quentin Crisp (1910-99), British writer, raconteur and author of *The Naked Civil Servant*. He described himself as 'one of the stately homos of England' and delivered an alternative 'Queen's Speech' at Christmas.

Government

To be governed is to be watched over, inspected, spied on, directed, legislated, regimented, closed in, indoctrinated, preached at, controlled, assessed, evaluated, censored, commanded; all by creatures that have no right, nor wisdom or virtue... O human personality! How can it be that you have cowered in such subjection for sixty centuries?

Pierre-Joseph Proudhon (1809-65), French social theorist.

Post-Cold War world

I say one evil empire down… one to go.

Michael Moore, contemporary, US documentary maker
and scourge of corporate America.
His films include *The Big One*.

A well-trained dog

Circus dogs jump when the trainer cracks the whip, but the really well-trained dog is the one that turns somersaults when there is no whip.

George Orwell (1903-50), British novelist, essayist and social commentator.

Wealth

God grants wealth to those coarse asses to whom He gives nothing else.

Martin Luther (1483-1546), German rebel theologian, opposed to the corruption and abusive power of the Catholic Church.

Piety

know there are people in this world who do not love their fellow man, and I HATE people like that.

Tom Lehrer (b. 1928), US humourist and songwriter.

Racial equality

I knew someone had to take the first step and I made up my mind not to move.

Rosa Parks (b. 1913), African-American woman who, in 1955, refused to surrender her seat on a segregated bus in Alabama to a white man. The incident helped kick-start the US Civil Rights movement. She later added, modestly: 'I'm just an average citizen. Many black people before me were arrested for defying the bus laws. They prepared the way.'

Y ou don't have to live next to me, just give me my equality.

Nina Simone (b. 1933), US jazz musician and civil-rights activist, singing in 'Mississippi Goddam'.

Free trade

If defending democracy, human values, and livelihoods is protectionism, then let us all proudly proclaim ourselves to be protectionists.

David C Korten, contemporary, Harvard-trained US economist who has become one of the sharpest critics of globalization and corporatism. His books include *When Corporations Rule the World*.

History

As long as someone else controls your history the truth shall remain just a mystery.

Ben Harper, contemporary, radical
US singer-songwriter.

Love

Let me say, with the risk of appearing ridiculous, that the true revolutionary is guided by strong feelings of love. Above all, always be capable of feeling any injustice committed against anyone anywhere in the world.

Ernesto 'Che' Guevara (1928-67), iconic Argentinean revolutionary and guerrilla leader who was second-in-command to Fidel Castro during the Cuban revolution. He was captured and executed in Bolivia.

To love without role, without powerplays, is revolution.

Rita Mae Brown (b. 1944), US novelist.

Nature

Let us not flatter ourselves for our human victories over nature. For every such victory, it takes its revenge on us. At every step we are reminded that we by no means rule over nature like a conqueror over a foreign people, like someone standing outside nature. But that we with flesh, blood and brain belong to nature and exist in its midst.

Friedrich Engels (1820-95), German political economist who with Marx co-authored the Communist Manifesto.

How to be saved

1 Let Jesus save you. **2** Come out of your blanket, cut your hair, and dress like a white man. **3** Have a Christian family with one wife for life only. **4** Live in a house like your white brother. Work hard and wash often. **5** Learn the value of a hard-earned dollar. Do not waste your money on giveaways. Be punctual. **6** Believe that property and wealth are signs of divine approval. **7** Keep away from saloons and strong spirits. **8** Speak the language of your white brother. Send your children to school to do likewise. **9** Go to church often and regularly. **10** Do not go to Indian dances or to the medicine men.

Mary Crow Dog (b. 1953), US Native American activist and writer of *Lakota Woman*.

Language

Explore the idea of what the language that women speak would really be if no one were there to correct them.

Hélène Cixous, contemporary, French feminist philosopher.

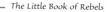

Memory

It's a poor sort of memory which only works backwards.

Lewis Carroll (1832-78), British mathematician and author of *Alice's Adventures in Wonderland*.

Delicate industrialists

Surely there never was such a fragile china-ware as that of which the millers of Coketown were made. Handle them ever so lightly, and they fell to pieces with such ease that you might suspect them of having been flawed before. They were ruined, when they were required to send labouring children to school; they were ruined, when inspectors were appointed to look into their works; they were ruined when such inspectors considered it doubtful whether they were quite justified in chopping people up with their machinery; they were utterly undone, when it was hinted that perhaps they need not always make quite so much smoke. Whenever a Coketowner felt he was ill-used – that is to say, whenever he was not left entirely alone, and it was proposed to hold him accountable for the consequences of any of his acts – he was sure to come out with the awful menace, that he would 'sooner pitch his property into the Atlantic'. This had terrified the Home Secretary within an inch of his life, on several occasions.

Charles Dickens (1812-70), British novelist, writing in *Hard Times*.

Killing and dying

There are causes worth dying for, but none worth killing for.

Albert Camus (1913-60), Algerian-born novelist and essayist. Author of *The Rebel*.

Privilege

Those who take the most from the table, teach contentment. Those for whom the taxes are destined, demand sacrifice. Those who eat their fill, speak to the hungry, of wonderful times to come. Those who lead the country into the abyss, call ruling difficult, for ordinary folk.

Bertolt Brecht (1898-1956), German dramatist, poet and committed Marxist.

Mind

The most potent weapon in the hands of the oppressor is the mind of the oppressed.

Steve Biko (1946-77), South African
anti-apartheid activist.

McDonald's

It just really stuck in the throat to apologize to McDonald's. I thought it was them that should have been apologizing to us – well not us specifically, but to society for the damage they do to society and the environment.

Helen Steel, contemporary, a British gardener who with postal worker Dave Morris was sued for libel by McDonald's in 1995. The pair stood up to the burger giants, refused to apologize, and defended themselves during the longest civil libel case in British history. The judge upheld their claims that McDonald's exploited children in advertising; falsely advertised its food as nutritious; was responsible for cruelty to animals and was strongly anti-union.

True democracy

My notion of democracy is that under it the weakest shall have the same opportunities as the strongest... No country in the world today shows any but patronizing regard for the weak. Western democracy, as it functions today, is diluted fascism. True democracy cannot be worked by twenty men sitting at the centre. It has to be worked from below, by the people of every village.

Mahatma Gandhi (1869-1950), Indian independence leader.

Evil

Nothing is easier than to condemn the evildoer, nothing is harder than to understand him.

Fyodor Dostoyevsky (1821-1881), Russian novelist, author of *Crime and Punishment*.

Anger

If you're not angry then you're just
stupid
or you don't care
how else can you react when you know
something's so unfair
when the men of the hour
can kill half the world in war
or make them slaves to a superpower
and then let them die poor.

Ani DiFranco, contemporary, US singer-songwriter.

Insurrection

Insurrection is an art, and like all arts it has its laws.

> **Leon Trostsky** (1870-1940), Russian Communist
> revolutionary, assassinated by Stalin.

Heroism

I am a hero with coward's legs.

Spike Milligan (b. 1918), British humourist,
animal rights activist.

Order

Watch out for the fellow who talks about putting things in order! Putting things in order always means getting other people under your control.

Denis Diderot (1713-84), French philosopher.

Revolutionary's dues

The first duty of the revolutionary is to get away with it.

Abbie Hoffman (1935-89), US radical left-wing political activist, anti-Vietnam campaigner, founder of the Yippies, author of *Steal This Book*.

Globalization

What is called 'capitalism' is basically a system of corporate mercantilism, with huge and largely unaccountable private tyrannies exercising vast control over the economy, political systems, and social and cultural life, operating in close co-operation with powerful states that intervene massively in the domestic economy and international society.

Noam Chomsky (b. 1928), US linguist, political analyst and leading critic of corporatism and globalization.

Dictators

Worshipping a dictator is such a pain in the ass.

Chinua Achebe (b. 1930), Nigerian author of the colonial and post-colonial experience. His books include *Things Fall Apart* and *Anthills of the Savannah*.

Good soldier

I spent 33 years in the Marines. Most of my time being a high-class muscle man for Big Business, for Wall Street and the bankers. In short, I was a racketeer for capitalism. I helped purify Nicaragua for the international banking house of Brown Brothers in 1909-1912. I helped make Mexico and especially Tampico safe for American oil interests in 1914. I brought light to the Dominican Republic for American sugar interests in 1916. I helped make Haiti and Cuba a decent place for the National City Bank boys to collect revenue in. I helped in the rape of half a dozen Central American republics for the benefit of Wall Street…

Smedley D Butler (1881-1940), Major General in the US Marines turned political activist.

Voting

*I*f voting could change the system, it would be illegal.

Theodore Adorno (1903-69), German philosopher, sociologist and musicologist.

*T*he vote, I thought, means nothing to women. We should be armed.

Edna O'Brien (b. 1936), Irish novelist.

Neutrality

Washing one's hands of the conflict between the powerful and the powerless means to side with the powerful, not to be neutral.

Paulo Freire (1921-1997), Brazilian philosopher and pioneer educator 'for social change'.

Truth telling

During times of universal deceit, telling the truth becomes a revolutionary act.

George Orwell (1903-50), British novelist, essayist and social commentator.

Beauty

A h, but in such an ugly time the true protest is beauty.

Phil Ochs (d. 1976), prolific US protest
and folk musician.

Health

It is no measure of health to be well adjusted to a profoundly sick society.

Jiddu Krishnamurti (1895-1986), Indian spiritual philospher.

Winning

First they ignore you. Then they laugh at you. Then they fight you. Then you win.

Mahatma Gandhi (1869-1950), Indian independence leader.

Each generation

Each generation must, out of relative
obscurity, discover its mission, fulfill it,
or betray it.

Frantz Fanon (1925-61), Martinique-born psychiatrist,
philosopher and political activist. His experiences of
the Algerian independence struggle prompted him to
write *The Wretched of the Earth*.

Class

While there is a lower class, I am in it. While there is a criminal element, I am of it. While there is a soul in prison, I am not free.

Eugene Debs (1855-1926), US trade unionist and political leader, helped found the Socialist Party of America.

Extremism

Extremism in the defense of liberty is no
vice; moderation in the pursuit of
justice is no virtue.

Cicero (106-43 BC) Roman writer, senator and
outspoken critic of power, executed for
offending the ruling triumvirate.

Enemies

Yes, I know my enemies
They're the teachers who taught me to fight me
compromise conformity assimilation
submission ignorance hypocrisy brutality
the elite
all of which are American dreams.

   Zach de la Rocha (b. 1970), US rock singer, activist
       and Zapatista support organizer.

How to succeed in revolution

We must utilize surprise, cunning and flexibility; we must use the strength of the enemy to undo him, keeping him confused and off-balance. We must organize with perfect clarity to be utterly unpredictable. When our enemies expect us to respond to provocation with violence, we must react calmly and peacefully; just as they anticipate our passivity, we must throw a grenade.

Stokely Carmichael (1941-1998), Trinidad-born US civil-rights activist and Pan-Africanist, credited with the slogans 'Black Power' and 'Black is Beautiful'.

The question

When I give food to the poor, they call me a saint. When I ask why the poor have no food, they call me a communist.

Dom Helder Camara (1909-99), radical Brazilian Catholic priest and Liberation Theologian.

Change it!

How can you sit so comfortably with the indifference that you're evidencing with this tragedy [famine in Africa], when you could, in fact, take some part of that tragedy and fix it and make a difference? Not all of it. Don't sit there and be overwhelmed by the enormity of the problem. Just pick out that portion which is yours, and kick butt. Go out there and make a difference. Change it. Change it. Change it!

Harry Belafonte (b. 1927), US singer and civil-rights activist. Played a central role in organizing the USA for Africa charity recording 'We Are the World'.

Agitation

So long as the water is troubled it cannot become stagnant.

James Baldwin (1924-87), US author, spokesperson for black and gay issues.

Men: a proposal

Life in this society being, at best, an utter bore and no aspect of society being at all relevant to women, there remains to civic minded, responsible, thrill-seeking females only to overthrow the government, eliminate the money system, institute complete automation and destroy the male sex.

Valerie Solanas (1936-88), US feminist, author of the SCUM (Society for Cutting Up Men) Manifesto. Also notorious for shooting (but not killing) Andy Warhol.

Sanity

Contrary to popular belief, conventional wisdom would have one believe that it is insane to resist this, the mightiest of empires… But what history really shows is that today's empire is tomorrow's ashes, that nothing lasts forever, and that to not resist is to acquiesce in your own oppression. The greatest form of sanity that anyone can exercise is to resist that force that is trying to repress, oppress, and fight down the human spirit.

Mumia Abu-Jamal (b. 1954) US journalist, environmentalist and death-row prisoner. He was convicted of killing a police officer.

War

When the rich wage war, it's the poor who die.

Jean-Paul Sartre (1905-80), French writer and philosopher.

Optimism

I am an optimist – with no timescale.

Amos Oz (b. 1939), Israeli novelist who
has campaigned eloquently for
the rights of Palestinians.

Prostitutes and wives

Prostitutes don't sell their bodies, they rent their bodies. Housewives sell their bodies when they get married – they cannot take them back.

Florynce Kennedy (1913-2001), US feminist
and pro-abortion activist.

Logos and no logos

Ethical shareholders, culture jammers, street reclaimers, McUnion organisers, human-rights hacktivists, school-logo fighters and Internet corporate watchdogs are at the early stages of demanding a citizen-centred alternative to the international rule of the brands… as global, and as capable of co-ordinated action, as the multinational corporations it seeks to subvert.

Naomi Klein (b. 1970), Canadian anti-globalization activist and writer of *No Logo*.

Life and death

I postpone death by living, by suffering, by error, by risking, by giving, by loving.

Anaïs Nin (1903-77), French-born novelist and diarist.

You don't get to choose how you're going to die, or when. You can only decide how you're going to live. Now!

Joan Baez (b. 1941), US folk singer associated with the protest movement.

Fitness

Contrary to popular cable TV-induced opinion, aerobics have absolutely nothing to do with squeezing our bodies into hideous shiny Spandex, grinning like a deranged orangutan, and doing cretinous dance steps to debauched disco music.

Cynthia Heimel, contemporary, US journalist.

To win back my youth there is nothing I wouldn't do – except take exercise, get up early, or be a useful member of the community.

Oscar Wilde (1854-1900), Irish-born wit and playwright.

Experience

The notion of the universality of human experience is a confidence trick and the notion of a universality of female experience is a clever confidence trick.

Angela Carter (1940-92), British novelist.

Western civilization

The truth is that Mozart, Pascal, Boolean algebra, Shakespeare, Parliamentary Government, baroque churches, Newton, the emancipation of women, Kant, Marx, Balanchine ballet et al, don't redeem what this particular civilization has wrought upon the world. The white race is the cancer of human history, it is the white race, and it alone – its ideologies and inventions – which eradicates autonomous civilizations wherever it spreads, which has upset the ecological balance of the planet, which now threatens the very existence of life itself.

Susan Sontag (b. 1933), US writer and critic.

Crime

We make our own criminals, and their crimes are congruent with the national culture we all share. It has often been said that a people get the kind of political leadership they deserve. I think they also get the kind of crimes and criminals they themselves bring into being.

Margaret Mead (1901-78), US anthropologist.

To the end

I hope to die at my post: in the streets or in prison.

Rosa Luxemburg (1871-1919), Polish-born revolutionary who set up the Spartacus League, later to become the German Communist Party. She was murdered by army officers.

Writing

Socrates wrote nothing. Christ wrote nothing.

Iris Murdoch (1919-99), Irish-born
philosopher and novelist.

I would venture to guess that Anon, who wrote so many poems without signing them, was often a woman.

Virginia Woolf (1882-1941),
British novelist and feminist.

Revolutionaries

The most radical revolutionary will become a conservative the day after the revolution.

Hannah Arendt (1906-75), German-born political philosopher. A refugee from the Nazis, she is best known for her analyses of fascism and totalitarianism.

Every revolutionary ends as an oppressor or a heretic.

Albert Camus (1913-60), Algerian-born French writer, author of *The Rebel*.

Theft

I asked a man in prison once how he happened to be there and he said he had stolen a pair of shoes. I told him if he had stolen a railroad he would be a United States Senator.

Mother Jones (Mary Harris Jones, 1830-1900), US pioneer labour organizer known for her feisty spirit.

To the full

Don't compromise yourself. You're all you've got.

> **Janis Joplin** (1943-70), US blues singer who took the male-dominated rock scene by storm.

My motto – *sans limites.*

> **Isadora Duncan** (1878-1927), US-born pioneer of modern dance who initially scandalized audiences with her idiosyncratic performances.

Age

Old age is no place for sissies.

Bette Davis (1908-89), US screen actor, known for
playing strong independent female roles.

Blasphemy

All great truths begin as blasphemies.

George Bernard Shaw (1856-1950),
Irish-born playwright.

Work

No man can call himself a liberal, or radical, or even a conservative advocate of fair play, if his work depends in any way on the unpaid or underpaid labour of women at home, or in the office.

Gloria Steinem (b. 1934), US feminist writer and editor, co-founder of *MS* magazine.

One of the symptoms of approaching a nervous breakdown is the belief that one's work is terribly important.

Bertrand Russell (1872-1970), British philosopher, mathematician and lifelong pacifist activist.

Racial discrimination

Sometimes, I feel discriminated against, but it does not make me angry, it merely astonishes me. How can any deny themselves the pleasure of my company? It's beyond me.

Zora Neale Thurston, contemporary, African-American writer and activist.

Sacrifice

Jesus died for somebody's sins but not mine.

Patti Smith (b. 1946), US punk rocker and poet.

The information age

Computers are merchandise. Treat them as such. Believe nothing you hear from people selling (and these days everybody is selling). Expect nothing to work as advertised... People who think education equals information have no idea what either information or education is.

Theodore Roszak (b 1933), US writer, critic and Neo-Luddite thinker.

Delinquency

Prisons are built with stones of Law,
brothels with bricks of Religion.

William Blake (1757-1827), eccentric British poet and
searing critic of early industrial capitalism.

Inquiring spirit

I will burn, but this is a mere incident. We shall continue our discussion in eternity.

Michael Servetus (1511-53), Spanish physician and theologian, commenting to judges of the Inquisition after being condemned to the stake as a heretic.

Marriage

Marriage is the only adventure open to the cowardly.

Voltaire (1694-1778), French writer and philosopher.

A husband is what is left of the lover after the nerve has been extracted.

Helen Rowland, contemporary, US journalist.

Happiness in marriage is entirely a matter of chance.

Jane Austen (1775-1817), British author of *Pride and Prejudice*.

The World Bank

The main problem at the [World] Bank has to do with its faulty vision of development – the spreading of Western over-consumption worldwide.

Herman Daly, contemporary, US leading economist, formerly of the World Bank, now one of the foremost critics of economic orthodoxy.

Resistance

I never steal, always cross the street in the right place. A whole lot of nice things I do. But I'm against the Government. I'm definitely against the Government!

Dita Sari, contemporary, Indonesian activist and champion of exploited women textile workers. In 1999, at the age of 21, she was imprisoned for leading thousands of workers against Suharto's dictatorship.

Military glory

He who joyfully marches to music rank and file, has already earned my contempt. He has been given a large brain by mistake, since for him the spinal cord would surely suffice. This disgrace to civilization should be done away with at once. Heroism at command, how violently I hate all this, how despicable and ignoble war is; I would rather be torn to shreds than be a part of so base an action. It is my conviction that killing under the cloak of war is no different than murder.

Albert Einstein (1879-1955), Austrian-born physicist.

My song

My song is not for the rich
no, nothing like that
My song is the ladder
we are building to reach the stars.

> **Victor Jara** (1932-73), Chilean folk musician
> who was murdered by Pinochet's military.
> These words come from 'Manifesto'.

About New Internationalist Publications

New Internationalist is a publications co-operative based in Oxford,
UK, with editorial and sales offices in Aotearoa/New Zealand,
Australia and Canada. It publishes the **New Internationalist** magazine
on global issues, which has 65,000 subscribers worldwide. The **NI** also
produces the One World Calendar, Almanac and Greetings Cards, and
publications such as *Eye to Eye: Women* plus food books including *The
Spices of Life* and *Vegetarian Quick & Easy* – cooking from around the
world. New books from the **NI** include the *No-Nonsense Guide* series,
with titles including *Fair Trade, Climate Change* and *Globalization*.

For more information write to:

Aotearoa/New Zealand PO Box 4499, Christchurch.
newint@chch.planet.org.nz

Australia and PNG 28 Austin Street, Adelaide 5000, South Australia.
helenp@newint.com.au

Canada and US 1011 Bloor Street West, Toronto, Ontario M6H 1M1.
nican@web.net

United Kingdom 55 Rectory Road, Oxford OX4 1BW.
ni@newint.org

See all our products on the NI website at:
www.newint.org